Celebrate!

Id-ul-Fitr

Mike Hirst

WAYLAND

Other titles in this series:

CHINESE NEW YEAR   CHRISTMAS   DIWALI

A note on this book:
The symbol ﷺ is used each time the Prophet Muhammad ﷺ is mentioned. This means 'Sallallahu alaihi wa sallam' (peace and blessings of Allah upon him).

Cover photograph: A child and her mother opening their Id Mubarak (Happy Id) cards.

Title page photo: Children in Saudi Arabia wearing their best party clothes for Id-ul-Fitr.

500 414891

All Wayland books encourage children to read and help them improve their literacy.

✓ The contents page, page numbers, headings and index help locate specific pieces of information.

✓ The glossary reinforces alphabetic knowledge and extends vocabulary.

✓ The 'finding out more' section suggests other books dealing with the same subject.

Find Wayland on the Internet at http://www.wayland.co.uk

Editor: Philippa Smith
Designers: Tim Mayer and Malcolm Walker

First published in 1999 by Wayland Publishers Ltd
61 Western Road, Hove, East Sussex BN3 1JD

© Copyright 1999 Wayland Publishers Ltd

British Library Cataloguing in Publication Data
Hirst, Mike
  Id-ul-Fitr. – (Celebrate!)
  1. Id-ul-Fitr – Juvenile literature
  I. Title
  297.3'6

ISBN 0 7502 2529 7
Printed and bound by Eurografica, Italy

This book is based on the original title **Id-ul-Fitr** in the *Festivals* series, published in 1996 by Wayland Publishers.

Picture acknowledgements
Eye Ubiquitous 5 right, 23 bottom; Sally and Richard Greenhill 22, 24; The Hutchison Library (Kerstin Rodgers) 17; Christine Osborne 4 top, middle and bottom left, 5 left, 7 top, 12, 16, 19 (both), 21, 26 (B. Hanson), 27; Peter Sanders *cover*, title page, 4 bottom right, 6, 7 bottom, 8, 9, 11 (both), 13, 15, 18, 20 (both), 23 top, 28, 29; Trip 10 (Nasa), 25 (F. Good). Border and cover artwork by Tim Mayer.

Contents

Id-ul-Fitr Around the World   4

What is Id-ul-Fitr?   6

The Prophet Muhammad ﷺ Fasts   8

The New Moon of Id   12

Id Begins with Prayers   16

Giving to Others   22

Celebrations   24

Muslim Festival Calendar   28

Glossary   30

Finding Out More   31

Index   32

Words that appear in **bold** in the text
are explained in the glossary on page 30.

Id-ul-Fitr Around the World

◄ Britain
Many **Muslims** now live in Europe. Their families have moved from countries in Africa and Asia.

▲ Pakistan
People often watch polo matches in the Id holidays.

▲ Egypt
Muslims go to a **mosque** for prayers at Id.

▲ Kenya
Women reading from the holy book of **Islam**, called the **Qur'an.**

◀ <u>China</u>
Muslims give money
to the poor at Id.

▲ <u>Uzbekistan</u>
In the month before
Id, Muslims read all
of the Qur'an.

What is Id-ul-Fitr?

The word 'Id' means 'joy' or 'happiness'. Id-ul-Fitr is a very happy festival for Muslim people.

Id happens at the end of a month called **Ramadan**. Ramadan is a quiet, serious time. During this month, Muslims pray a lot. They think about how to be good people. They think about **Allah** too. (Allah is the Muslim name for God.)

▲ Id balloons and sweets for sale outside a mosque.

Id Song

In India, Muslims sing a song about Id. It begins:
'Id has come, Id has come,
It makes us happy, it makes us happy.'

Muslims belong to a religion called Islam. They try to live good lives, and do what Allah wants them to do. They find out about Allah by reading their holy book, which is called the Qur'an.

Id-ul-Fitr is a time for Muslim people to meet and celebrate. Families and friends join in special meals and parties.

▲ The Qur'an teaches Muslims how to lead good lives.

►Making sweets to celebrate the end of Ramadan.

7

The Prophet Muhammad ﷺ Fasts

In early times, wise men called **prophets** told Muslims what Allah wanted them to do. Then in 570 **CE**, a very special man called Muhammad ﷺ was born. He was the last and most important prophet.

Muhammad ﷺ lived in the desert. He often went to quiet places to think and pray. One day, he was sitting at the top of a mountain when an angel called Jibril came to him.

▼ Mount Hira, where the angel Jibril visited Muhammad ﷺ.

The angel read messages to Muhammad ﷺ. Muhammad ﷺ remembered them and later said them out loud to his secretary. Then Muhammad's ﷺ secretary wrote the messages down. This is how Allah gave the Qur'an to his followers.

▲ This is a copy of the Qur'an. It is written in a language called Arabic and the pages are decorated with patterns.

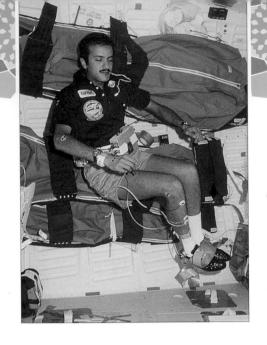

The angel Jibril first visited Muhammad ﷺ in the month of Ramadan. Muhammad ﷺ made this a special time, called a **fast**. During a fast, people stop eating and drinking. Muhammad ﷺ told people very carefully how to fast.

▲ Prince Sultan-bin-Sulman on a spacecraft during Ramadan.

At Ramadan, Muslims get up before sunrise, and eat a small breakfast. They also drink a lot of water, because they will not eat or drink anything else during the daytime. They end the fast each day after sunset.

Ramadan in Space

The Muslim astronaut Prince Sultan-bin-Sulman went on a space mission during Ramadan. But he fasted even when he was in outer space.

◄ A Muslim family eat a small meal after dark.

During Ramadan, Muslims read the Qur'an out loud. The book is in 30 parts, and people read one part each day of the month.

The 27th night of Ramadan is called Laylat-ul-Qadr. People say special prayers on this day, because it is when the angel Jibril first visited Muhammad ﷺ.

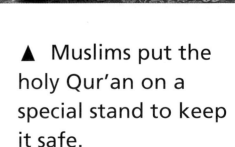

▲ Muslims put the holy Qur'an on a special stand to keep it safe.

Starting and Ending the Day

To start the fast each day, a Muslim says a special prayer.

To end the fast each day, a Muslim drinks water and eats three dates.

The New Moon of Id

Muslims measure the months by the shape of the moon. There is a thin, new moon at the start of each month. The moon gets bigger in the middle of the month, and smaller again at the end. Some months last for 30 days, others for 29.

◄ Lights decorate a mosque at Id-ul-Fitr.

In Ramadan, Muslims watch the moon carefully, and count the nights as they go by. As the moon gets smaller, the month is nearly over. When a new moon begins, a new month, called Shawwal, starts. The first day of Shawwal is Id-ul-Fitr.

When Muhammad ﷺ was alive, people also used the moon and the stars to find their way on long journeys.

▲ A moon with this thin, crescent shape is called a new moon.

Desert Travel

In the desert, people often travel at night. This is the coolest time of the day. Light from the moon helps people find their way.

The Muslim Calendar

In the Muslim calendar, there are 12 months. Each month has 29 or 30 days. Most years have 354 days.

Countries in Europe and America use a different calendar, and a year usually has 365 days. For this reason, Muslims who live in Europe and America celebrate Id at a different time each year. For example in 1997 Id was in February, but in 1999 it was in January. Every year it is at an earlier time.

The centre of Islam is in the city of **Makka**, in Saudi Arabia. As soon as religious leaders in Makka see the new moon of Shawwal, they send messages all around the world. Id has arrived.

Some religious people feel quite sad that Ramadan is over. Ramadan is a time when Muslims can feel close to Allah.

For other people the end of Ramadan is a busy time. They have to shop and prepare food for the Id festival. In Muslim countries, shops stay open all night in the last few days of Ramadan.

▲ At Makka, people gather to watch for the new moon of Id.

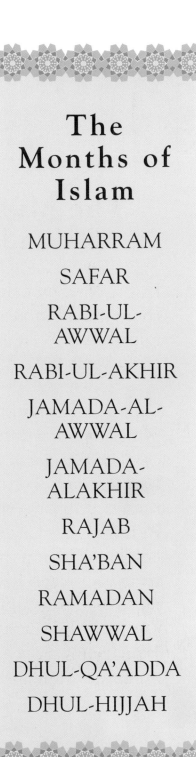

The Months of Islam

MUHARRAM

SAFAR

RABI-UL-AWWAL

RABI-UL-AKHIR

JAMADA-AL-AWWAL

JAMADA-ALAKHIR

RAJAB

SHA'BAN

RAMADAN

SHAWWAL

DHUL-QA'ADDA

DHUL-HIJJAH

Id Begins with Prayers

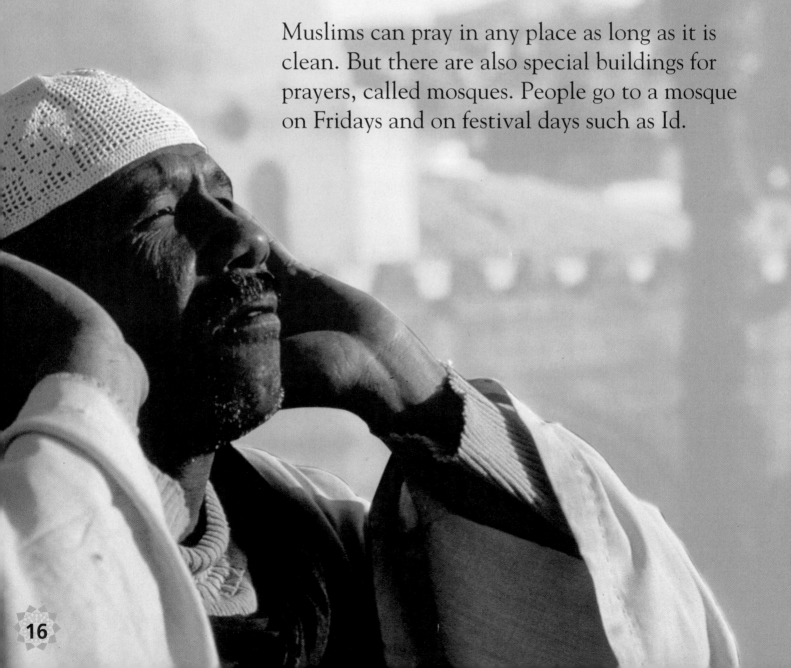

▼ The first prayer of the day is at sunrise.

The festival of Id always begins with prayers.

Prayers are very important for Muslims. Muhammad ﷺ taught his followers to pray five times every day.

Muslims can pray in any place as long as it is clean. But there are also special buildings for prayers, called mosques. People go to a mosque on Fridays and on festival days such as Id.

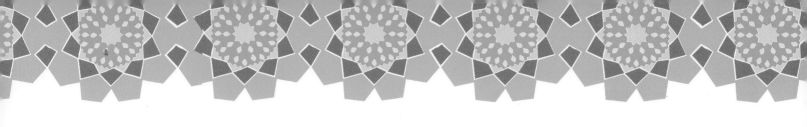

A man with a strong voice sings out to people from the mosque when it is time for prayers. He is called a **mu'azzin**. He stands at the top of a tall tower called a **minaret**. His voice travels to all the houses in the village or area near the mosque.

▲ Muslim women climbing the steps of a mosque in India.

The mu'azzin begins the call to prayer with these words:

'God is great! God is great!
There is no God but Allah.'

At the first prayer of the day, the mu'azzin says: 'Prayer is better than sleep!'

Everybody goes to their mosque at Id. They wear their best clothes.

Women wear clothes that cover most of their bodies. They only show their hands and faces. Men have to cover the lower parts of their bodies, but they usually cover the top parts too.

It is important to be clean before prayers. Every mosque has a place to wash. Muhammad ﷺ taught his followers exactly how to wash.

▲ Muslim girls in Saudi Arabia wear new party clothes at Id.

◄ Many Muslims have a special mat or rug to stand on when they say their prayers.

People also take off their shoes when they go into a mosque. This is to show respect for the holy place.

When they pray, Muslims turn to face the holy city of Makka. They also stand and kneel in special ways.

▲ Washing before prayers.

At Id-ul-Fitr a religious leader called an **Imam** says the prayers at a mosque.

After the prayers, people wish one another 'Id Mubarak', which means 'Happy Id' in Arabic. There are food stalls outside the mosque. People spend time talking to friends before they go home with their family.

▲ Sharing food with other Muslims is an important part of the Id festival.

◄ Muslims from different countries greeting each other at Id.

At Id, Muslims think about people in their family who have died. They often visit the graves of dead relatives.

Muslims believe that they will go to Paradise after their death if Allah wants them to.

Muslims come from many different countries. But all Muslims learn Arabic. They use the language to read the Qur'an and to speak to other Muslims.

▼ A Muslim graveyard. All Muslims are buried with their head towards Makka.

Giving to Others

Muhammad ﷺ wanted everybody to share in the festival of Id. So when Muslims go to the mosque at Id, they take a special gift called zakat-ul-fitr.

In some places, Muslims give food to the mosque. This food makes an Id feast for poor people.

In other countries, Muslims give money for their **zakat**. Religious leaders use the money to pay for the Id feast. Muslims who live in rich countries often send zakat money to poor Muslims abroad.

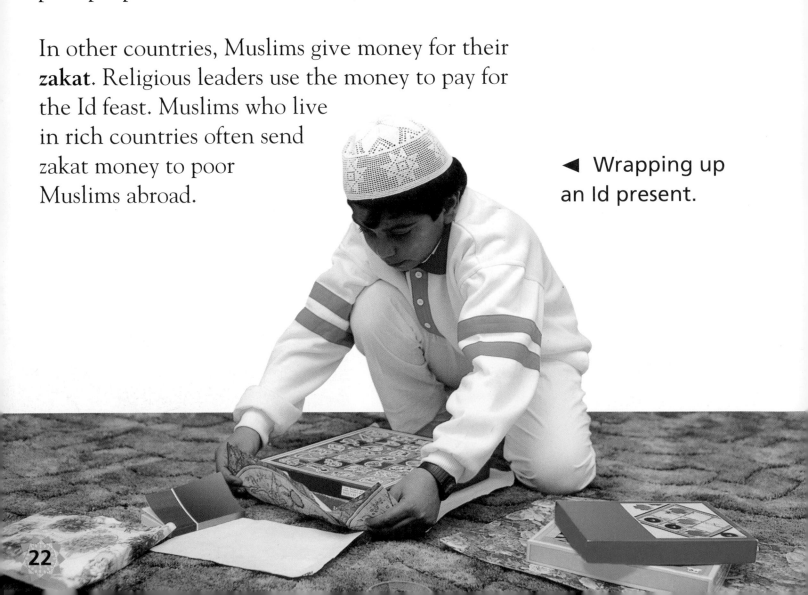

◀ Wrapping up an Id present.

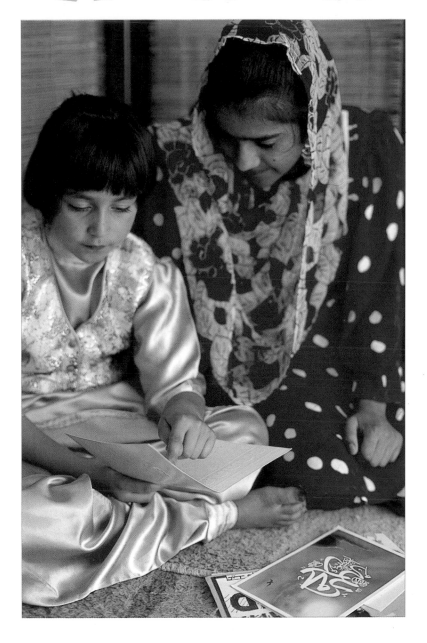

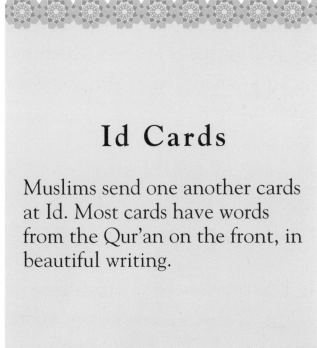

Id Cards

Muslims send one another cards at Id. Most cards have words from the Qur'an on the front, in beautiful writing.

◀ Opening Id cards.

People also give Id presents to their friends and family.

▶ Children save up their pocket money to give zakat at Id.

Celebrations

In Muslim countries, the Id holiday lasts for three days. But Muslims who live in America and Europe normally take just one day off school or work.

At family parties, people eat special food. Meat is always **halal** meat. This means it has been killed in a way that is explained in the Qur'an.

Muslims do not eat pork. They do not drink alcoholic drinks such as beer and wine.

◄ Muslim children take an Id meal to the table.

In different countries, there are different types of Id festival. In the Middle East and North Africa, people go to watch horse races or camel races.

▲ Children in Pakistan watch a game of polo wearing their best clothes.

In Iran, Pakistan and Afghanistan, a sport called polo is popular. Players ride on ponies. Two teams try to hit a ball into a goal using long sticks.

▲ In Africa, men wear long robes and turbans at the Id festival.

In India and Turkey, there are markets at Id. Shops sell jewels and sweets to give as Id presents. Sometimes, actors and acrobats come to the markets too.

In Africa, people celebrate Id by singing and playing folk music.

Other countries have competitions for reading the Qu'ran. Some people can read all of the book out loud from memory.

Muslims respect people who know the Qu'ran very well.

▼ Camel races take place at Id in Saudi Arabia.

Muslim festival Calendar

There are six big festivals every year in Islam.

Al Hijra

Al Hijra is the first day of Muharram. This is New Year's Day for Muslims. On this day, Muslims meet in groups and tell stories of how Muhammad ﷺ and his followers moved from Makka to start new lives in the city of Madinah.

Meelad-ul-Nabal

Muhammad ﷺ was born on the 12th day of Rabi-ul-Awwal. This is his birthday.

◄ Muslims celebrating the festival of Meelad-ul-Nabal.

Lailat-ul-Isra

The Qu'ran tells how Muhammed ﷺ visited heaven on the night of the 27th of Rajab. 'Lailat-ul-Isra' means 'night of the journey'.

Laila-ul-Barh

This festival happens just before Ramadan. It is the time when Muslims ask Allah to forgive them for anything they have done wrong.

Two weeks after Laila-ul-Barh, Muslims begin a month of fasting. This is called Ramadan.

Id-ul-Fitr
Id begins at the end of Ramadan. It celebrates the end of the Ramadan fast.

Id-ul-Adha
This festival also happens at the end of Ramadan. Muslims remember a story in the Qu'ran about the prophet Abraham. Abraham always did exactly what Allah wanted him to do. At this festival, Muslims think about how to give everything they have to Allah.

▲ All Muslims try to visit the holy city of Makka. Going to Makka is called a hajj, or pilgrimage. In Makka everyone visits a monument called the Ka'aba.

Glossary

Allah   The Muslim name for God.

CE   Common Era. This is a way of writing dates that is used by all countries today.

fast   To give up eating and drinking for a time. Muslims fast from dawn to sunset during the month of Ramadan.

halal   The Qur'an tells Muslims how to kill animals for meat. Meat killed this way is called halal meat.

Imam   A Muslim religious leader.

Islam   The Muslim religion.

Makka   A city in present-day Saudi Arabia. It was also the birthplace of Muhammad ﷺ.

minaret   A tall tower in a mosque. The mu'azzin stands at the top of the minaret to call people to prayer.

mosque   A building where Muslims meet to worship Allah.

mu'azzin   The man who calls people to pray together at a mosque.

Muslims   People who follow the religion of Islam.

prophets   Men who give messages from God to other people.

Qu'ran   The Holy Book of Islam.

Ramadan   One of the months in the Islamic year. Ramadan is a time for prayer and fasting.

zakat   Muslims use this word to mean 'giving to the poor'.

Finding Out More

BOOKS TO READ

Feasts and Festivals by Jacqueline Dineen (Dragons World, 1995)

Holy Cities: Makka by Shahrukh Husain (Evans, 1999)

My Muslin Faith by Khadijah Knight (Evans, 1999)

My Muslim Life by Riadh El-Droubie (Wayland, 1997)

Out of the Ark: Stories from the World's Religions by Anita Ganeri (Macdonald Young Books, 1997)

Ramadan & Id-ul-Fitr by Rosalind Kerven (Evans, 1996)

The World of Festivals by Philip Steele (Macdonald Young Books, 1996)

What Do We Know About Islam? by Shahrukh Husain (Macdonald Young Books, 1996)

OTHER RESOURCES

Festival Worksheets by Albany Bilbe and Liz George (Wayland, 1998): 25 pages of photocopiable, copyright-free worksheets on the topic of festivals, together with teachers' notes and topic web.

USEFUL ADDRESSES

The Islamic Cultural Centre,
146 Park Road, London NW8
Tel: 0207 724 3363
Web site address: www. ramadan.co.uk

The Islamic Book Centre,
120 Drummond Street, London NW1
Tel: 0207 209 0710

The Festival Shop,
56 Poplar Road, Kings Heath,
Birmingham BI4 7AG
Tel: 0121 444 0444 Fax: 0121 441 5404
The Festival Shop stocks all kinds of educational material relating to festivals.

MUSEUMS

The following museums have exhibitions of Islamic art and culture. Always check that the exhibitions are open before you visit.

The British Museum,
Great Russell Street,London WC1B 3DG
Tel: 0207 636 1555
Web site address: www. british-museum.ac.uk

The Victoria and Albert Museum,
Cromwell Road, London SW7 2RL
Tel: 0207 938 8500
Web site address: www. vam.ac.uk

Index

Africa   4, 25, 26
Allah   6, 7, 8, 9, 14, 17, 21, 29, 30

calendar   14, 15
cards   23
China   5
clothes   18, 25, 26

Egypt   4

families   4, 7, 11, 20, 21, 23
fasting   10, 11, 29
festivals
  Al Hijra   28
  Id-ul-Adha   29
  Laila-ul-Barh   28, 29
  Lailat-ul-Isra   28
  Meelad-ul-Nabal   28
food   7, 11, 14, 20, 22, 24, 26, 30

hajj   29

Id Mubarak   20
Imam   20
India   17, 26
Islam   4, 7, 14, 15, 28, 30

Jibril   8, 9, 11

Kenya   4

Laylat-ul-Qadr   11

Makka   14, 15, 19, 21, 28, 29, 30
minarets   17, 30
moon   12, 13, 14, 15
mosques   4, 6, 12, 16, 17, 18, 19, 20,
  22, 30
Mount Hira   8, 9
mu'azzin   17, 30
Muhammad ﷺ   8, 9, 10, 11, 13, 16,
  18, 22, 28, 30

Pakistan   4, 25
prayer   4, 6, 8, 11, 16, 17, 18, 19, 20
presents   22, 23, 26
prophets   8, 29, 30

Qu'ran   4, 5, 7, 9, 11, 21, 23, 24, 27,
  29, 30

Ramadan   6, 7, 10, 11, 13, 14, 28,
  29, 30

Saudi Arabia   18, 27, 30
Shawwal   13, 14, 15

washing   18, 19

zakat   22, 23, 30
zakat-ul-Fitr   22